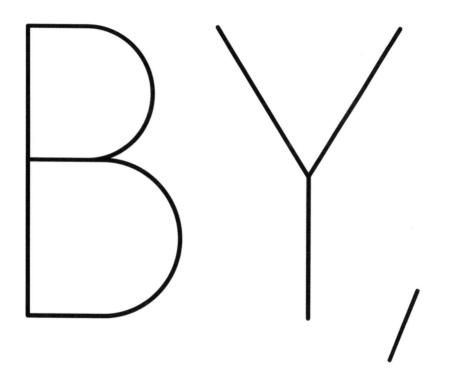

Wave Books

Seattle/New York

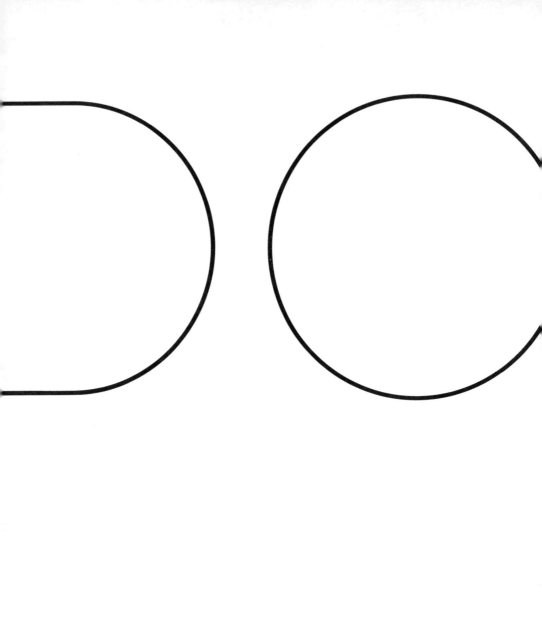

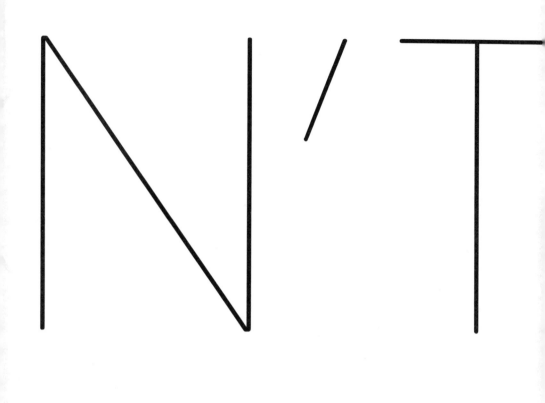

Chelsey Minnis

Published by Wave Books

www.wavepoetry.com

Copyright © 2018 by Chelsey Minnis

Wave Books titles are distributed to the trade by

Consortium Book Sales and Distribution

Phone: 800-283-3572 / SAN 631-760X

Library of Congress Cataloging-in-Publication Data

Names: Minnis, Chelsey, 1970– author.

Title: Baby, I don't care / Chelsey Minnis.

Description: First edition. | Seattle : Wave Books, [2018]

Identifiers: LCCN 2017060733 | ISBN 9781940696713

(limited edition hardcover) | ISBN 9781940696720 (trade pbk.)

Classification: LCC PS3613.I654 A6 2018 | DDC 811/.6—dc23

LC record available at https://lccn.loc.gov/2017060733

Designed and composed by Quemadura

Printed in the United States of America

9 8 7 6 5 4 3 2

Wave Books 072

For Steve

|

||

III

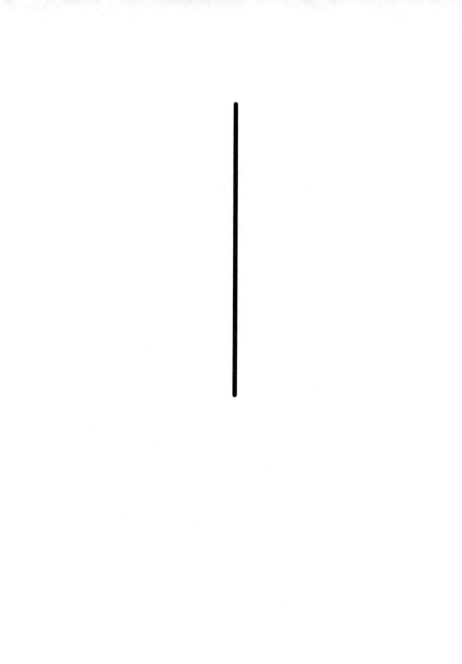

INTRODUCTIONS

Everyone knows dates and locations and things like that.

But I don't know anything like that.

Now let's have a kiss.

I can send you a bill for the poem.

It costs a meat locker full of rubies.

I'm going to do a lot of tough thinking.

You're furnishing the liquor.

Let's mess up our lives the right way.

There is something in the mind called the soul.

But we've got to beat everyone using only our good looks.

What's the use of thinking?

Some people can't come along.

Sometimes I don't talk to anyone, I just fixate on their necktie.

The kind of person I am, you don't hurt the other person.

But your perfume climbs on like a tarantula.

Am I laughing?

On the contrary.

Please let me think of the right self-reprimands.

I assure you, this will be a conventional poem.

Now let me introduce you to a hungry tigress, me.

What do you want with me?

I'm just a dirty little shoplifter.

I'm like a woman in a sequined gown in a dark cave.

Can you tell me I'm worse than others?

OK, yes, I'm worse than others, but can you say I'm the worst
    of all?

Now let's be reasonable with ourselves.

If you show me a man in a turtleneck sweater on the beach,

then that is beyond my resistance.

If you show me a liquor cart on wheels,

I will just climb on.

Who am I?

Someone who kisses your shoulder when they're not supposed to.

I'm wearing high heels by the pool so that makes everything OK.

Now don't be charming, darling.

There could be a lot of smashed vases in our future.

What should I do? Mind my manners?

I'm the type of person to lose an emerald ring.

I might drop it in my champagne and drink it.

How can I be such a swine?

Oh, darling. I hate to be thirsty.

8

Let's have a drink, medicinally.

I'll stand on the couch and introduce myself.

This isn't a drink, it's pure leopard sweat!

You shouldn't be allowed to run around with me.

I'll only give you a good time.

9

LAZINESS

Into this hostile world, I bring a special laziness.

I like to go swimming after cocktails!

Then I put on sunglasses and write a poem.

I guess I better make it hot and shiny.

This can only lead to compliments.

As usual, I've had my usual success.

Now let me send myself some flowers.

Mother was a famous bareback rider and Father was a pool shark.

It makes the others crazy, the way I lounge!

Someday, I'll be taken to jail in my tennis shorts.

13

I've always wanted a pearl stomacher.

What's to be done?

Take a memo—

one of us has got to be sensible.

Well, it's not going to be me.

I've always wanted to be the daughter of a wealthy communist.

I'm not surprised!

I'd be surprised to be surprised.

Here's my plan—

let's fall asleep on chaise longues while we wait for some money.

14

First of all, do you have any money?

Sometimes, I feel a slight warmth about money.

Baby, I might not be any good!

The only thing I do is write down words.

I make it special though, don't I?

I wonder about things, but not too much!

You must understand the great laziness.

And don't you feel colossal?

Forget about the math, baby.

By all means, let's get drunk in a bar with a coat of arms on the sign.

15

VIPs

This is a matter of life or death, probably death.

Your bullet is very close to my heart.

You're way off base, darling.

Let's put some ice on our fingers.

By ice, I mean diamonds.

You know how I am.

Oysters for lunch, dinner, and breakfast.

A broken heart is not for me.

Now, don't I want some mink?

Don't tell me you're a bloody communist!

19

When you say it with feeling, then you're wonderful.

Going out of my mind wouldn't be hard.

You need to be kicked under the table.

Let's go sell another polo pony.

I've worn my diamonds down to the bone, darling.

I'm afraid someone's not going to give me my favorite thing!

Then I would bite their head or face.

This could be a long turnaround.

Baby, don't be gruesome!

I only wanted one stuffed grizzly bear in my study, not two.

20

I like to scream in a satin bed

and get a baby bunny as a present.

I can't stop thinking of myself and what might be to my own

advantage!

For example, I love to go to bed sober,

which means I have to start drinking early.

Don't keep saying "down the hatch" all night long.

Something matters, but what is it?

A window with a very long fall underneath?

One time someone refused to give me a pink topaz and I fainted.

Let me be the first to pour your tears down the drain.

21

SUCCESS

Am I ever going to stop doing as I wish?

If you gave me thirty lucky breaks, I could succeed!

Write me a good line or I'll zip up my dress.

That's the way I feel about it.

Maybe I leave a lot of chances on the table.

Listen, junior, and learn.

You want to know what poetry is? A flea circus.

That's a point that'll take a lot of arguing.

But don't let's get sticky about it.

Kill the people, darling.

25

Never again will I write you some trash!

Like you know I can.

I can write this now or later.

I can hurt you with a poem or hurt you in bed.

Either way, you're getting treated right.

That's the last you'll see of that thousand.

But don't let that bother you.

It's a fair start.

You and I got to have an understanding.

I think I'm quite the most adorable swindler I've ever met.

26

I am a thing. A thing to be loved!

Now go ahead and scamper away.

Don't you know how to criticize the world?

I'll take you out back and show you some poems.

I never want to get ahead, that's all.

Life might not be as fun as I think it is.

But who cares?

Everyone has to get wised up sooner or later.

Now come back from the war and kiss me.

Then go get in your breadline.

27

LARCENY

Someday, I might try to think about another person's feelings.

Only after I do some petty larceny.

Let's get in the same racket.

The racket is dirty talk.

Let me know when we start understanding each other.

Look, it's been very hard to puppeteer myself

all these years!

I desire to have a true humility,

but it's hard,

and men are no help.

I'm pretty good at the ukulele.

What's to be done?

Might I ask for a clearer definition of "subversive activity"?

Now isn't this something?

I broke the strap of my evening gown.

And you think I'm helpless.

On the contrary, I sympathize with you deeply.

If that's the way you want it.

I can see you're going to be a hard case.

Of course, you do have the build for it.

32

You have a pretty low opinion of me, haven't you?
I did something wrong, once.
Oh, but that was years ago.
Don't get sentimental, darling.
What's new in the world of slander?

If you love me, baby, tell me all about it.
It's charming when you lecture me sternly.
Darling, the ice would melt in my veins.
You and your diamonds.
Anytime I want anything from you I'll take it.

33

HANDSOME

I like this kind of buildup.

When you can only see the back of his head.

It's a pure gorgeous back of the head.

Now, the poem is over.

Well, be happy about it.

Let's discuss our minor grievances.

One minor grievance is a handsome man.

I want to look at him but I don't want to listen to him.

Am I allowed to say anything? Or should I just go lie down in my
    coffin?

Now, please don't underreact.

You're a fine-looking man with his hair rumpled.

But my thoughts are freight trains.

I want to be magnificent, but you must be magnificent with me!

You don't end a poem like this.

Let's go get some smoke in our eyes.

What makes me so terribly sleepy is your constant handsomeness.

I don't want to crush a baby chick in my hand!

But I can't help it.

Tell me. Are you a peaceful man?

Let's not talk about the moon and stars.

Baby! I need to put my head back and think.

Let me just slick my hair back and think.

Baby, it's so sexy to think.

Why don't you try it?

You're the good-looking type. Too bad I don't like that type.

Let's get thrown into third class.

Let's wear satin robes and be unreliable.

I guess you mean something to me.

Enough to make me hurl a highball glass into the fireplace.

39

What are you? A male beauty?

Darling, I think you're abnormal.

Now let's have dinner every night and loads of beautiful luncheon.

Don't be riffraff, darling!

Then again, I like riffraff.

40

COMPLIMENTS

I told you once I was going to have to tell you something.

Well, this is it.

There's something about you that makes you a treat.

And there's something about you that makes you a louse.

Sometimes I ride the ferris wheel for hours not thinking of you.

I simply hate your simple guts.

So, why don't you sit next to me?

You're a terrific rosebud.

I think you are a priest smoking a cigarette.

If only I could forbid you some small happiness.

43

Please don't step on my accordion!

Let's have a drunken rumble & don't take it seriously.

I don't hate you, darling!

You happen to be a nice side of beef and you are a man.

But someday, someone might want to get witty.

I like you! Except on occasion.

I'm going to be sick & I am sick!

Now, let's pull the corkscrew out of our neck & keep going.

I don't know how good this is.

You can shake my hand, but don't hold it and pet it.

44

Why do you insist on breaking my tiaras?

Baby, it's not good for you to be so evil.

Darling, you have such a soft belly.

I always want to cut a soft belly, I can't help it.

No, don't try to get away.

Nothing's wrong with you, so, congratulations.

What will you do now?

Stand on the balcony looking good?

Nothing's wrong with you and I like it.

I'll take your silence as a non-goodbye.

45

ROMANCE

Let's stop shaking hands goodnight.

Let's be very nice to each other until one of us can't stand it.

Even though we have stolen each other's diamond clips.

First of all, I never think things over.

You're in the men's room and I'm in the ladies' room, and then we
both come out at the same time.

I'm going this way and you're going that way.

Want to make something out of it?

It would be, I understand, the very height of folly.

Let me tell you about love.

Anyone could take an overdose of this stuff.

49

Darling, I want you to buy me a car in my favorite color.

My favorite color is wine.

Also, give me a flower in a paper cup.

You shouldn't ever leave me.

That's a way to get your tuxedo cried on.

Darling, why don't we share adjoining rooms?

Let's get stewed to the eyeballs.

Now let's have a fight while I brush my hair.

Can you be trusted?

So why don't you come over to our table and introduce yourself?

50

What are you hatching up in that pretty head of yours?

I guess I sized you up wrong.

You look at me so gently.

Want to play for keeps?

The grenades are in the champagne bucket.

Now blow out your candles.

I have a feeling I could go for you.

I guess it's like the sexual equivalent of a flamethrower.

What are you going to do?

Complain about the heat?

51

FUN & GAMES

I want to wear a satin evening gown and drive a steamroller.

Shouldn't someone toast to my health?

Darling, are you killed?

It's a sad thing to run a man into the ground, but I've done it.

Because I burn so brightly in bed, darling.

Should we give in to our kindness and humility?

Don't ask me. I'm just a little chiseler.

What are you going to do? Shoot the jukebox again?

Don't be so terrific!

I'm trying to squander my sex appeal, but it's terribly hard.

Someone can't help it if they are an immoral princess.

What's it like to be good?

Let's run around together.

You could do something unforgivable while wearing a gorilla suit.

Don't make me any bedtime promises.

You're a very nice article of merchandise.

Now go ahead and scamper away.

I'm going to lie down on the floor and laugh.

I'm frigid, baby!

Let's eat cocktail wieners together & be friends.

56

Tonight I'll wear the burnt-orange gown.

You know I look well in burnt orange.

Baby, it's natural to want a thousand dollars!

Why don't you ever say a dirty thing to me?

Darling, you're undersexed.

Let's fall in love,

just the three of us.

Let's be objectionable and immoral and utterly no good.

Should we lie down right here and fight about it?

Now bring me those dance instructions.

I merely love you.

But you want to go to blazes.

From now on, I'm just out for the ride.

I like it when you're a tramp, but even more than that, I like it
when I'm a tramp.

Let me assure you I have no qualifications.

I like it when two men take off their dinner jackets and fight.

I like all the wrong moves.

I have a dirty mind, but what do I do with it?

Maybe it's useless, like a bleeding fin.

I walked through all the rooms of the sex club but I couldn't see
the fun in it.

Remember that time we had sex in front of the tigers?

Now let me think it over.

Does anyone supervise me?

Something's wrong with me and I like it.

How much is this little poem going to cost me?

Look, there's no reason to be kind.

I want you to give me a positive feeling

in my pants.

And if you're a very bad lamb,

I'll give you a very rare treat in the form of a mink panty.

59

GOLD DIGGER

It's yes or no, isn't it?

After all, I'm a big girl.

And famished for diamonds.

That means it's bedtime.

Now, where did I hide that champagne?

Baby, why don't you give me an oil well or something?

Now, don't get mad, baby!

What do you think I want? Money?

Yes, I want money.

63

I've been so terribly broke all my life.
You see, I haven't your advantages.
I don't approve of me either!
Why don't we all go to bed?
Gentlemen, nothing would please me more.

I need to lie down on the carpet and rest.
Then let's get dressed up and go out.
Let's wear too much confounded lip rouge!
I can amuse you for months.
But how many swimming pools can I have?

64

Less flattery and more cocktails.

Eggs, bacon, and ham in large quantities.

A 30-piece string orchestra.

It's simple arithmetic, darling.

I haven't even pity for you.

Other people think they have it,

but you have it.

Now I'm going to climb into a bikini.

Darling, let's be poor!

But first, let's be rich.

65

Now, don't kiss my forehead again.

Now, dole out some pearls.

Come over and drag me around because I like it.

But if you really love me,

you're dropping diamonds from your crop duster.

66

BOREDOM

You're a pretty attractive burglar.

Can't you do me a lot of favors?

But let's not have any lines of dialogue between us!

I'm trying to make you last a long time.

You see, my boredom is legendary.

Oh darling, it's so dull trying to stay alive.

You know who we are?

We're the flops.

We're Mr. and Mrs. Flop.

Try not to talk when you're sober, darling.

69

Let's be at our most charming.

I'll go first.

On the other hand,

let's not say anything and see if we like it.

If we do, let's try it again.

Let's tussle.

Your brains against my brains.

But then again, forget it.

Look, just pry the gemstones out and get going.

Tomorrow's another nothing.

70

Everything's sort of boring and yet I feel sort of ravishing.

Let's not be innocent.

I have to climb out the porthole because I hate you, darling.

You're a good person . . .

Goodbye!

71

GOODBYE

We were pals, if that's what you mean.

Well, no one's indispensable.

I may as well be nice to you.

I'm going to give you up.

Now, that's a fancy name for murder.

Couldn't we be cockeyed fools for once?

Let's wear our black velvet shorts.

I need some cold cuts and champagne.

Baby, please stop winking.

But first, goodbye.

75

Let us have a cutoff.

And quick as the devil!

Don't put your fist to your mouth and cry.

Look, all our broken parts are scattered around the room.

We have to reassemble ourselves into separate robots.

Now even though we're a couple of rats, I think we're marvelous.

I'm having a swell time. Now let me alone.

Goodbye, monster.

It's no use chasing me anymore.

I was born into this merry-go-round.

76

I get lonelier and lonelier and then I eat all the pink capsules for
    dinner.
How come I never get any telegrams?
It's surprisingly easy to be enraged in a ruffled dress.
Look at yourself in the reflection of your flask.
You used to be a hobby of mine.

People in their nightgowns, smoking cigarettes,
they give great speeches.
I like it like upside-down sunsets.
I like it like a mess of emeralds.
I like it when you gesture from your forehead, "So long!"

77

DARLING

Oh, it's you.

I never could resist anything that belonged to someone else.

I suppose you feel the same.

That's a very promising black eye.

If you want one, fix it yourself.

You wear a big, gold belt buckle with your name on it.

Now, I really like your eyes when they look at me with that look.

The one that is so fair-minded.

It's dangerous like a very powerful doorbell.

Or a portrait covered with a blanket.

83

You didn't lock your door.

You never were very particular about your associations.

Does it give you a lovely guilty feeling?

To me you're a national disgrace.

Please act accordingly.

I didn't hit you very hard.

It all depends what you want out of life.

Never mind talking.

I know I'm a bad woman.

I think you'll find it to our mutual benefit.

84

Sure, I'm decent.

I'll have to try that sometime.

Don't shout, darling. I'm not used to it.

I need my hand back now.

When I don't like something, I give it back.

You find it amusing to tempt me?

How right you are.

The word is "incautious" and I am.

You might be bluffing, but I'm not.

You wouldn't happen to have any extra pajamas?

Don't play cards with me, darling, I'm a cheat.

It's true. I'm weak.

I'd like to take a bite out of you.

How about your wife? Is she broad-minded all of a sudden?

If you're going to leave, then why don't you hurry?

86

YOU

Rather dangerous playmate, aren't you?

Example A: Your brain.

Think you can start a fire with it?

Now don't be a killjoy.

I love a psychotic.

What are you? Some kind of chaser?

Do you want to make love?

How about a couple of steaks

and a certified check for $1,000?

Maybe I'll let you stand next to me and catch my fleas.

89

You've got to love someone abominably, don't you?

Then why are my cheeks all wet?

I am ready for my row of drinks!

This poem is so fucking showy.

But you're going to take it.

You're a tigerskin rug of a man.

You're just some man I beat at chess.

So why can't we leave each other alone?

Now fix me a drink.

Later we can try some wrestling moves.

90

Your thoughts and my thoughts simply don't agree.

But it's amusing to hit you with my armcast.

Shouldn't everything be perfectly all right?

Don't be silly.

Nobody puts me in checkmate.

What are you? Some guy with the million-dollar hands?

Everyone is getting progressively outranked.

I don't intend paying any more of your gambling debts.

I merely think you're a terribly attractive person.

Someone's got to be held tight.

91

I love a pet chimpanzee, but I love you as well.

I love you more than crystal ashtrays.

Here's the terrible nod that means you're displeased.

Why don't you kiss me then?

Mash me to a pulp.

92

BARGAINING

Did you ever try eating your cake?

Listen here, I'm crazy about you.

You haven't sold a diamond mine, have you?

Shut up, will you, darling?

You're still thinking in dollar signs.

Look, just because I always complain and never keep my chin up,

is that any reason to think I won't make a good wife?

How I love to be selfish!

That's why I drop my fur coat on the floor when I walk into the
    room.

Yes, the loathsome groove of money!

95

I can run circles around someone running in circles.

Now pull the venetian blinds and we'll talk.

This business requires a certain amount of finesse.

I'm going to tell a very long, very dirty joke.

This could be hard on your pocketbook.

I'll admit I'm in love with you.

I'm the dust under your feet.

So, why don't you give me a string of ponies?

I'm sorry, darling, of course. There's no sense in overplaying it.

We're all that kind.

96

What are your conditions, baby?

Don't lead someone on a merry chase.

Maybe you should give me a bigger diamond.

I can offer you my charm as security?

We'll be wiped out, darling.

You and I don't like each other.

It's likely to wear off any minute.

I wish you were hard and cold and calculating.

I've got a funny feeling way down inside,

I don't want that ten grand.

97

Now, I might be strictly ornamental.

This is highly agreeable as long as I am paid in gems.

Let's have a nebulous goal, like the goal to be blasé.

Darling, pull yourself together.

I swear I have never cared about those pearls.

I wanted to get under that hard shell of yours, darling.

It's all a lot of mush.

What makes you think this is going to be a big scene?

Let me tell you about love.

We'll be paying installments for the rest of our lives.

BUSINESS

Let's settle our accounts.

Let's conduct our interviews from the bathtub.

Now hand me my robe.

There's a pretty good chance I love you,

but I'll have to take it up with my board of directors.

What in the name of heaven can they do?

The contract's signed.

Anyway, I like to be pawed over.

I believe in keeping up your standards at night.

Don't be such a sterling character, darling.

101

There are a lot of compliments lying around.

Why don't you give me some?

You're the kind of darling I hate.

Now let's get ritzy.

I'm a pair of diamond earrings away from sleeping with you.

I just want to get a smell of the money.

I'm fed up with this kind of living.

Will you help me with the zipper, darling?

I never *can* get a zipper to close.

I think that's good business.

102

I'm the kind of person who breaks heirloom ashtrays.

I'm the kind who whirls a jumbo globe.

Have I said something awful? Why not?

I like it when I have a bad idea.

Why don't you make me your beneficiary, darling?

Don't throw the typewriter at me!

I only sit on the *arms* of chairs.

No one tells me to cheer up.

I can give you more than a moment's boredom.

And then comes the dawn, but I don't know what that means.

103

SEDUCTION

Babe, I'm thinking something very sloppy.

Do you have any folding money?

What's the point of all those beige tuxedos in your closet?

Start sinking your kisses into my mouth.

Don't let me die of thirst, baby.

The thing I need to do is get myself ruined.

Are you going to take this abuse?

Come over & give me some atmosphere.

Come over & we can stare at each other for a while.

Don't catch a little fish and throw it back again.

107

I only need a little encouragement to keep me going.

Now, don't fog up your reading glasses.

How about a fistful of opals?

I love it when you get high-minded.

Darling, I would never strike first.

I hate you, baby.

I want to be your nuisance.

If you don't like it, then why don't you pay for some charm lessons?

First, we have to insult each other's butlers.

Then the downhill hallway leads to my bedroom.

108

Let's stop being so damn polite.

You've got what I want, all of it.

But I hate to be proposed to.

I expect I like you better than any man I've ever known.

After all, it's my funeral.

109

ARRANGEMENTS

Let's make a mess of everything.

Surely we can come to an understanding?

You're a man in a tuxedo in a tree.

Let's play the scene how it's written.

Be a darling and get it, won't you?

Don't be so hard to love.

I like you and all the rest of it.

But I'm going to throw you out of my kitchen.

Don't ruin the ideal arrangement with your broad shoulders.

Why not kiss in a doorway if you can?

113

It's a nice view, baby. What does it mean?

You find me too rough to play with?

I'm of no particular importance.

Why don't you go make love to your wife?

The outstanding novelty of the year.

Church! It bores me.

I want to live in a system with you.

Let's wear lots of gold jewelry and pajamas.

I withdraw that slap and all the drinks I threw in your face.

All that remains of the business is romance.

114

Are you going to be vexed with me?

Well, let me have it on credit.

Well, my loneliness might come round to visit.

Aren't you going to ask me down for the week-end?

I could always use an extra man.

Why don't you give me some refreshing diamonds?

We're a fine couple of tramps. So what?

Let's get dressed up and stay home.

You can't do a thing to me. Not a thing.

It's a very slow getaway, darling.

DEATH

I want to shoot myself!

But how will I ever get hold of a gun?

Now, I am thinking too hard.

It makes my cheeks hot.

This is no time to be brainy!

Death? I don't love it.

I already know how everything is.

That's why I wear a bikini and ride a horse.

Are we going to get along?

The word for what I want is "money."

119

I like diamond-cut emeralds and emerald-cut diamonds.

Darling, it's not so hard.

Give me the fancy talk now.

Later you can cover my body with a sheet.

Much later.

Life is life and then the florist delivers you flowers.

Everyone's going to croak, aren't they?

Now is the time to get soberer and soberer.

Let's get very organized with our compliments.

I only want one bad time and it's you.

120

Don't go and die in a boating accident.

Let's fall in love on the high dive.

What *about* life? Is it all bad?

What's your policy on champagne?

I enjoy kidding myself, but only at the beginning.

Dear beauteous death,

Oh no you don't!

And yet, I can't help being fond of you.

My eyelids are getting heavy.

Well, don't look so pleased.

Death isn't really important, is it?

Don't let's have any goodbyes.

Now, this is a reckless waiting.

I don't know what we're waiting for.

First thing you know, we'll be sober.

122

DRINKING

Now look here, I feel swell.

We've been doing some high-class guzzling.

May I ask why the honor of this visit?

Are we sleeping or dancing?

Lunch is poured.

Aren't I some kind of human being?

Or am I just a dead swan?

Baby, why aren't we drunk?

Am I swaying?

Well, stop playing that crazy xylophone.

Are you a man or an iceberg?

If you're afraid of me, then go lock yourself in a cage.

Don't try to give me any peace and quiet.

Now it's time for everyone to get their drink poured.

Bring me a fresh leopard!

You've completely gone out of my mind.

I think it ought to have a very healthy effect on me.

You think a kiss from a smooth operator means anything?

How about a little drink?

Now, that should have been the first thing you said.

126

Someone says they're going to buy you a drink but they just *pour*
    you one.
Please don't shout after I've had my daiquiris!
I like to curl up on the couch in high heels.
I love you, darling, but don't you think it's immaterial?
Dynamite couldn't get me out of this chair.

I've tapered down to two quarts a day now.
Isn't it wonderful?
My whole outlook on life has changed.
Licentious, profane, obscure, and contrary to the good order of
    the community.
Who wouldn't come to their senses?

127

Now, let's crawl out of the cocktail lounge.

Why is everyone turning into their own stool pigeon?

Don't be one of these charming depressives.

Let's find out if we're a brilliant success.

All the objections are on one side.

128

FIGHTS

Point of information: What do you know about anything?

I'll give you extra time to figure it out.

No, I'm not going to cry.

I'm going to smash the geraniums.

Do you mind, darling?

I like it when you shake your fist at a painted portrait.

May I ask why you're so terrible?

I love you but you want to go to blazes.

Have you ever even tasted my tears?

The empty champagne glasses were waiting beautifully.

131

Don't look at me with that sparkle.

I don't like it.

Everyone shouldn't ruin everything.

I never win an argument, but there are other things in life.

Does anybody ever get that look out of their eyes?

I've had the right attitude once or twice.

I nearly went out of my mind.

What are you? A perfect rat?

I adore rats. Rats are sweet.

Now, let's have some yelling.

132

Now I'm going to stay dumb.

I'm going to need some help.

Baby, why don't you give me some money so I can get rich?

Oh, how many times I've hurt you!

And each time is precious to me.

Darling, this is a cylindrical satin sofa cushion.

I'm going to beat you with it.

Now, a lot of people don't know what I'm talking about.

That's what's so wonderful.

I'm afraid I'm going to have to accept that free ticket out of town.

133

Bulletin: You're no good.

I don't care who catches it.

It's a swell night for a cry.

That's KO with me.

Let's have ringside seats.

Bulletin: You're still no good.

I think you're the most no-good person I've ever known.

And that concludes tonight's sermon.

I know what you're thinking.

Maybe we'd get somewhere.

134

THREATS 1

Now I'm going to measure you for a suit.

And send you home to your mother.

Do you think you're any good?

Let's not be lightweight.

There's a luger in the bureau.

Wouldn't I?

I figure one of these days you might have a weak moment.

You see, I've really known you for years and years.

If you ever come within throwing distance again,

many happy returns, baby.

137

I always did like saying goodbye to husbands.

A certain feeling comes over me.

You don't seem to appreciate my methods.

OK. You win all the marbles.

I warned you to have nothing to do with me.

I'm not determined.

I've never been determined.

Now all the gentlemen will become nervous.

Can anyone blow money like I can?

Maybe I want your treehouse to burn.

138

And you needn't take that injured tone with me.

I know I did everything wrong.

Isn't it wonderful?

You've always been very fair in your judgments.

That's what you are, you know, a blind kitten.

You need a priest to hand you a beer and a cigarette.

You can drink the beer with the blood running down your face.

You're so handsome it's a shame.

It makes me want to murder some pigeons.

If I could ever help you, I'd fall in love with you.

REGRET

Sometimes I yearn for something better.

Don't take any notice of it.

Got a drink handy?

A little $1,800 birthday present?

I give it all back to you, including the yacht.

I'll never forget the night I stole your star sapphire cufflinks.

What are you? Some kind of innocent bystander?

There's such a thing as being too smart.

It's a lot of fun.

Supposing I don't want to live on memories?

143

Maybe I wish the past never happened.

Maybe I'm the wrong kind of stinker.

Now I'm going to open the shades.

I don't care for you,

but if you're going to walk around in feathers you deserve to be
loved.

You're some kind of handsomeness.

What are you going to do? Forcefully deny it?

I miss your boring, dominant lectures.

Do you miss my hatefulness?

A bad time was had by all.

144

Thank you for the truth, bitter as it is.

Perhaps we shall meet again.

Naturally, there's a long pause.

Now we are getting somewhere.

I'm practically there.

145

THREATS 2

Have you got a knife suitable for throwing?

I suppose I should thank you.

I was a good girl before I went to pieces.

You'll be good and sorry for that someday.

My dear, how can you doubt me?

I'm your enemy, aren't I?

Then why can't you give me aid and comfort?

We wouldn't have to strain ourselves.

This is what you'd call a physical attraction.

You have pretty good reflexes for an old man.

149

Someone takes your cigarette and

throws it on the ground and kisses you.

And you think you will go up against me?

Are you still that way?

Like a tiger sleeping under a baby's crib?

Whatever it takes to get a guy like you, I got.

Maybe it's because I'm so hard and tough.

We'll talk about that in the morning.

Isn't it marvelous the way we see eye to eye on everything?

Very well. If you choose to play the leopard, I will hunt you like a

    leopard.

150

I'm sorry you have to leave so soon.

You cheap little sensationalist!

I want you to be awfully happy.

This is nice and friendly, isn't it?

I have so few cherished grudges.

Go ahead. Slap me.

It's been a long day and I'm thirsty.

So why don't you get the blazes out of here?

Since you won't tell me, I'll tell you.

It's either a rowboat proposal or a murder.

Do you mean to say I'm going to die?

That's out, as far as I'm concerned.

Now, don't frown.

Our sense of humor always differed.

See you in church.

152

MURDER

Henceforth, murder.

A lot of good that will do you.

It's not in my line, darling.

You wouldn't be human if you didn't tingle a little bit.

Great heavens, what have I done else but?

Is there anyone to turn to?

You know I hate your singing.

Let's have a conversation in the fur refrigerator.

I'm a bad person but it doesn't matter.

You should be kind to your butcher.

155

I'm going to feed you to my goldfish.

No one should question that.

I don't get tough, darling.

I like to eat sweets in bed while wearing feathered dressing gowns.

Still, you might want to do what I tell you.

Now, be quiet and row me across the pond.

Did anyone ever tell you you row beautifully?

Did anyone ever try to kill you in a rowboat before?

This is the best nightmare.

Darling, the bathtub's running over.

You love me but you don't love my singing.

Why don't you ruin everything then?

Go ahead. Show me the clouds.

This would have been the perfect murder

if only you hadn't left a thumbprint on my glass eye.

Will you greet me with a knife then?

This makes everything ginger-peachy.

I'm really a very shallow person.

I love fireflies, mockingbirds, and pink sunsets.

I'm sorry I couldn't be saved.

157

I don't want any reasonableness with you.

I want to tell you something as I block your sunlight.

Many things should be said to you in doorways.

It's time to start crying but you don't realize it.

You see, I'm the type of person who would hurt a fly.

158

NERVES

If you come in here I'll scream!
And me with a beautiful hangover.
Suppose I have a nervous breakdown?
Shall I tell you something confidentially?
I don't mind if I do.

Look, baby, I want to be your dinner companion and that's not all.
I want to be your personal lemon squeezer.
I feel like a real sicko today.
Darling, this doesn't mean anything.
It's just a bit of stylish crawling.

161

I need psychiatric help. I rate pretty high there.

You know, in many ways I'm a terrible girl.

My attitude is one of complete optimism.

Do you intend going on?

I'm going to tear you apart and throw the pieces to the lions.

I'm sorry for slapping your face!

And now, let me begin 77 sunsets without you.

Let me whisper into your dictaphone,

"I murdered my pet canary."

Behold my dazzling mental illness like a chandelier.

Darling, I think you're my husband.

And this is the golden breakdown.

Or else some kind of mental leopardskin.

Anyway, I never mean anything I say on a yacht.

Now what's the most important thing in the world again?

Let me give you my feedback.

My feedback is arf arf arf.

You wouldn't understand, of course.

Is there any hope that I was never born?

Finally, everybody gets the right idea.

163

Now we're going down to the bottom to see if we like it.

I'm going to maul your head with my words.

I'm going to gesture with a turkey leg while I argue during dinner.

This poem is a display case for expletives.

And all the babydolls have recorded cries.

I like to be very funny and charming, to a point.

What are these tears for, anyway?

Suppose I do have a nervous breakdown?

Well, strap on your diamonds.

Things generally move in that general direction.

164

BREAKDOWN

I may slit my throat.

Maybe I'd like a little poison, too.

Well, there you are.

But I'm no such thing.

Well, yes and no.

I know everything should be red velvet.

But life is a terrible thing.

See? The poem is rigged with a joke.

No more guns, darling.

I can open the window and let myself out.

Do I mean things or not?

The softness of importance.

It's just a little stick of dynamite.

Don't I realize it's not appropriate to jump out a window

or fall in front of a train in my mind?

Don't go into your office and shoot yourself!

It gets very noisy before you die and then it gets quiet as a pond.

If you ask me, it's a failed success.

A head of brains should only be destroyed by boat propellers.

Now go enjoy your hamburgers!

Lock the liquor cabinets!

Let's have my favorite thing, which is relief.

Let's try to be more adequate.

Can anyone stop this greatness?

Let's be crazy inside ourselves like mental French ticklers.

Well, gentlemen, it is beginning to make sense.

I've always been a little soft in the head.

Hurt me? You delight me.

I suppose I should thank you.

Here I was contemplating a nice juicy suicide.

169

THE END

Something tells me you love me.

How does it feel to have that at your feet?

Understand, this is the end.

Do you mind, darling?

You wouldn't mess up a girl's lipstick if it weren't important, would
you?

Let's you and me have a good cry.

I'm going to squeeze a few diamonds out of you and then let you go.

Every woman's entitled to her hot tears if she wants them.

It's not a state secret, darling.

That's the way they're wearing them this year.

173

You're damn right I got it annulled!

I did exactly what you would do.

I got cockeyed.

Never mind the jokes.

Next time you see me, I'll be crashing Rolls-Royces.

Baby, don't hit the bottle so hard.

I'm afraid for you, darling.

Darling, the snorting horse.

A murderer in a beret.

I remember it all now.

174

Do you have something in you that will make you stick?

It's just too funny, isn't it?

This goes, now and forever.

Chiefly, because I've loved you.

You've wasted an awful lot of genius trying to make a fool out of me.

$70,000 is a lot of money to pay for a pack of insults.

Just put it on your expense account, darling.

It's too late to explain.

May I make a suggestion?

Maybe we've jumped into too many fountains.

175

DEPRESSION

I'm fancy but I'm no good.

In order to be happy I have to sacrifice my misery.

My favorite suckling misery!

The only way to be happy is to listen to records while wearing
    kimonos.

There's no such thing as safety.

It's a confounded thing to be alive.

Let's go to jail.

Let's be king and queen of the dump.

Give me a kiss and then some kind of talk.

But not too much.

I'm very depressed as I blow on the party horn.

Are you going to give me civilized or uncivilized kisses at midnight?

Are you going to rip my dress

or maul the piano?

A very dangerous thing is an enormous clock.

Now let's be depressed in oversized sunglasses.

It's the only fun we have.

I see you have the appearance of a wife stealer.

Let's not be broke!

Let's hate each other with our minds, not our bodies!

Depressing things are not depressing!

The right kind of sadness only makes me happy.

Don't you get it like I do?

I say ha ha all the time in pure happiness.

Now let's go see what's buried in my tomb.

You can't do this to me just because I don't pay a few bills.

Now you've made me lose a good day's sleep.

What's a thing like comfort?

Is it a bullet-sized headache?

Baby, you can keep your trinkets.

183

RICH

Champagne, is it?

I guess you think I'm dumb.

How terribly thrilling.

Shall I tell you something confidentially?

I hope you choke on caviar.

You worship nothing but dough.

I say you're wrong.

Now stop throwing chairs.

I see a lot of begging in your eyes.

I don't like to mention it.

187

You have no idea how this "money money money" bores me.

You dirty capitalistic stool pigeon!

Who said I was going to rant and rave?

This is pointed at your heart.

You can take your choice.

I have all the modernized emotions.

But if there's one thing I hate, it's a showy proposal.

I only like clumsy affection.

Now pick through the jewels to find the larvae.

Every time you say "cheap" and "vulgar" I'm going to kiss you.

188

You know, money means very little to me.

It's a blind alley with a barred gate at the end.

I wasn't cut out for your way of living.

Just tell them politely I'm drunk in a gutter somewhere.

That's very often the case.

I'm sorry about your yacht.

And you with a beautiful hangover.

Go on. Bawl me out some more.

Should we both be naive?

What you need is a personally conducted tour through the gutters.

189

Darling, give me fleas!

I love a poor happiness.

Yes, I do want to live in a kennel!

Now let's teach each other something.

I'll teach you how to be sorry.

I'm going to walk around in my silk slip and make a structured
  argument.

There are lots of ways to go wrong, and I have only tried a few.

And that's why the heart is a swamp.

How do you make a million dollars worthless?

With love, baby.

190

GENTLEMAN

You had me on a merry-go-round for a while.

That was terribly decent of you.

I have to run along now.

I'm beginning to catch on.

You're a very good person but you can't get away with it forever.

I hate your insides.

Is this a time for frivolity?

Yes, of course it is.

Bring your whip.

You're not going to tell me that love is anything lasting.

193

But I don't want any common decency!

You're walking around blindfolded with a satin sash.

Now let's just happen to fall in love.

You've got the wrong girl.

I'm afraid I haven't attended Sunday school for many years.

What do you think I'm made of? Rainbows?

I think that's more in your line.

Quite a high type, aren't you?

Love has the right-of-way before everything.

You don't know what beds are for.

194

I'm nothing but a hotel thief.

Let's never forget it, ladies and gentlemen!

For all the things you've done,

I know I should hate you.

I guess that could be arranged.

I couldn't bring myself to play such a dirty trick.

Well, this *is* a surprise.

Now I *have* shocked you.

Don't waste your tears on villains like me.

Not the first thing in the morning.

195

Have the decency to know what you've done.

You aren't *a* heel. You're *the* heel.

Now let's stare at the pinball machines sadly.

Please give me every consideration.

I don't even know what a gentleman is.

196

PHILOSOPHIZING

Steve McQueen is a man who can wear a turtleneck.

Now, when he blinks it really means something.

Or maybe I just like a turtleneck sweater worn under a gun holster.

Does everyone get to think interesting thoughts, or just me?

I see how things might get to be too easy.

Let me tell you how I know things.

I just think about them very hard.

And then I get ideas.

And maybe they're the right ideas and maybe they're the wrong
    ideas.

Now can't you try that?

199

You're not very fond of me, are you?

You won't get away with it.

After all, what do you get by traveling the primrose path?

Oh, more dissipation?

I'll have to try that sometime.

I don't mind telling you I was holding my breath.

Not the chandeliers, darling!

Don't begin that sort of thing.

Sometimes, I wonder whether we're not living the wrong-way up.

I take it I've been a great moral lesson.

200

Don't kill someone with a paperweight.

Kill them with a paper

that has a heavy poem on it.

What is life? A catalogue of experiences?

Now what's a time and place compared to a strong feeling?

Something's better than an action. It's a word.

A word like a piano in a submarine.

What will you do? Fall asleep in your fur coat?

I won't even try to be civilized where you're concerned.

I like parties where half the people wear swimsuits and the other
    half wear tuxedos.

201

Well, *be* bored then.

But that's the point about this whole setup.

You can't fight boredom forever.

Now sit there and think that over.

And be sure you have a good time.

Is life a catalogue of experiences?

Maybe I don't understand.

I want an ashtray filled with diamonds.

I want gumdrop-sized emeralds.

Let's go through it again.

202

SHOWDOWN

You again.

I thought for one happy moment you'd come to attack me.

Assault with gun, bourbon, and a sports car.

You and I know better than that, don't we?

You'll never die yearning.

I guess I sized you up wrong.

How terribly thrilling.

I'll take that drink now.

That's not so very big, is it?

Guns make me thirsty.

205

Here's the small talk, baby.

Is it small enough?

I could have shot you twice already, with blanks.

What's your angle, baby?

I'm in the high part of your range.

What I like about you is you're rock-bottom.

I'm all right. I'm just dumb.

You're a kind of wrong-way person and I'm a right-way person.

Don't you like our little arrangement?

That pistol isn't necessary.

206

What are you, an old enemy?

Baby, it's only a scratch.

I wouldn't attach too much importance to something said in a
Panama cantina.

You mean a great deal to me.

For the right price.

I can add two and two, can't I?

You've been trying to make a tramp out of me ever since I've
known you.

Darling, I feel I can speak with perfect frankness.

You've got an awfully nice mouth.

For a minute, I was afraid.

ICEBERG

Why so talkative? Let's kiss.

You're a sweet-tempered little number.

I think we might like each other if we tried.

Come now!

Everything should burn like burning icebergs.

All of us are bad, but some of us are worse.

We don't have to strain ourselves.

Don't you understand?

I was born with the hope to be chaste.

But you play the violin so damnably . . .

211

It makes me jump into the fountain.

It makes me crack up inside, it really does.

You're handsome, but you don't give me anything I can use.

Let's have drinks in my room after church.

I love you or words to that effect.

Shall I go or wait long enough to get my face slapped?

It won't be a new sensation.

I wonder what the *nice* people are doing tonight.

You think I'm beaten, don't you?

Well, I can still lose money.

212

I'm dumb about money.
But I'm ready for a row of drinks.
It amuses me to make up dirty toasts!
Sadly, let me return your wallet.

I lost my head, darling.
Oh, what's the difference?
I'll never be a good Girl Scout.
Darling, let's be broad-minded.
Maybe we'll have our hangover at Niagara Falls.

213

ENGAGED

I haven't any beaus and I don't have any prospects.

I'm a social flop.

I hate it when my pens run dry.

I'd like some of that champagne soup.

Do you think there's a chance I could make you perfectly
miserable?

How are you going to do it? With an axe?

I gather you don't approve.

I have to tell you the truth regardless of what happens to the
furniture.

I'll put this in the form of a guarantee.

This is the end of my career as a heartbreaker.

217

Don't give me any healthy amusements.
Let's have some use for each other, at night.
You're a funny little man!
They'll deliver the telegram to your tent.
It says we are to be married at once.

Let's think separately about the same thing.
The one with the cage around the bed.
This green satin gown itches terribly!
Now give me every consideration.
I think I will make a very attractive widow.

218

I love you too, but let's not be sticky about it.

You have your racket and I have mine.

I'd say this calls for a medium-class celebration.

Are we engaged?

I'm afraid I wouldn't make a model prisoner.

This is the time to be congenial, but I can't make it.

I'm the type who never likes your type.

Don't you see?

We're filthy in love.

Let's get some rice thrown on us.

219

You never think of anything but topic A, do you?

I'd rather have a canary.

All right, suppose we were married.

Could it be that I got what was coming to me?

And that goes double for you.

220

LOVE

It was a very hot funeral.

Now put your hand on my knee, and I'll tell you all about it.

Are you going to take an attitude?

Instead, why don't you hold on to someone for dear life?

This fur coat can be easily kicked to the side.

You behave very decent for no good reason.

Is that any way to treat an old friend?

Shall I laugh at your convictions?

Give me the right-of-way, darling.

I love you, more or less.

223

What's all the shooting for?

You have money and I haven't.

I'm sure we're going to work out our little problem splendidly.

You can do me a great kindness.

That's what they tell me.

Haven't I got any pride?

I am not quite to the level I should be.

I am in love with a man wearing sock braces.

I am like a chimpanzee smoking a cigarette.

I wonder, is this the perfect drift?

224

Do you want to talk business, or do you want to play house?
Here's the fluttering money. Take it.
Darling, you've given me weeks and weeks of happiness.
Let's settle down, just the three of us.
You, me, and the tigers.

I'll yell at you while I take a bath.
Then we'll set up a card table in the bedroom.
There's no use ignoring the fact that my dinner party's ruined.
You won't mind if I say I think you're behaving rather badly?
I consider that highly commendable.

225

Shall I criticize you or will you criticize yourself?

I don't need a special reason to live.

Can you be saved? Or should you be pushed in the pool?

I love you, darling, I thought I should mention it.

I'll have to be brought to your funeral in a cage.

226

MARRIED

What do you mean by calling me a killer?

It's just a flesh wound.

I'm sorry I slept with your brother, but I simply had to.

It's all supposed to be velvet, is it?

Tell me why you're so hard to please.

One has one's shameful episodes in life, doesn't one?

I suspect you're a treasure.

I don't know why I tell you this except I tell you everything.

I guess I'm horribly in love.

I can't keep my mind on my cards.

229

Darling! Why must you lock your desk?

I'm sorry, but I want to be a nuisance.

Naturally, I'm going to smoke in my nightgown!

Have we lost all our loopholes?

When you said, "Fuck you," you should have said, "Fuck you,
  princess."

Darling, you know I hate you when you're sick.

That's natural.

What are you ever going to get out of me?

Besides juicy disappointment?

Now, take your spoonful of champagne.

230

Get this, you.

You don't say anything and you don't do anything.

Now, order me a sirloin steak for two.

Look, let's say all the nice things and let the other things rest.

Darling, play the piano for the tigers. They like it.

If you want to bother someone, bother me.

I'm for it.

What consequences?

I have a terrific effect on you, baby.

You look revoltingly happy.

231

Remember the time you smashed the gold-veined mirror tile?

I'm glad I never got used to anyone else.

Old husband!

I like you because you're old!

Now let my words flow into your ear trumpet.

I know there are some instants of happiness left!

Remember when we fought bitterly on the rescue boat?

Now, why didn't you let me wear my diamonds on the rescue boat?

Darling! I don't *have* any manners.

Are you going to let me talk, or are you going to keep kissing my
  chin?

232

Darling, I'm practically all right.

But how far does that go?

Are these the real pearls or the phonies?

If you're going to beat someone then I'm going to turn the radio up.

You're not the only ferocious lion in the house.

I'm nothing but a beautiful woman doing card tricks.

And you're nothing but a handsome bellhop.

Let's fight like two swans.

A certain amount of this is unpaid happiness.

Then we have to dance our way out of the enclosure.

233

GREATNESS

Late at night I become dedicated to greatness.

And I make it very fun.

Now I'm wearing an evening gown in the morning.

I've used up all my money.

So I've got to shell this poem out.

I can't have many things I like. For example, I can't have a pinto
    horse.

I apologize to my country for being bad at math.

I am getting self-incinerated by boredom, so that's fair.

In fact, I think this is the uppermost of boredom,

like a tiger chewing on a velvet sofa cushion.

237

I don't try to seem very intelligent anymore.

I am beyond such effects.

Like a false limb full of stolen pearls.

Do you want me to write a poem?

Then hold my flask.

I'm not a blooming wreck, if that's what you mean.

A thousand times I've almost decided to throw everything
overboard.

You mustn't get any silly ideas into your head about me.

I've never flopped on you yet, have I?

I'm a howling success, darling.

238

If someone's really happy, can they be no good?

Now don't start trembling without me.

I demand several pittances!

Don't worry. I've known myself forever.

One word of praise would cause me to act contrary to my own
  self-interest.

It's just a poem, not a platter of brains.

So don't give me any lucky breaks.

Is it our fault no one fawns on us?

Let's not get forced into the mirrored casket of greatness.

It's easier to write this than to write nothing.

239

I'm a stranger but not in my poems.

This is not an emerald mine.

It's for somebody alive!

The only real disgrace is the refusal to believe in or listen to your
fellow man!

Somebody better kiss me when I say that.

240

FAILURE

What's all this going to get you?

I can't see that you've made such a brilliant success of your life.

You might like it better my way.

I've got $100,000 on my mind.

Later, we can put ice packs on our heads.

We're old and unsuccessful but that's not so bad.

There's still a chance to be humble.

To be the most humble person who ever lived!

There's a chance for unselfishness.

A great unselfishness like a secret oyster.

243

Darling, don't be meaningful.

We should go back to our playpens.

Some people suffer too little.

It makes me sorry for them.

Look at me. I make a wonderful failure.

They haven't seen anything like me for 20 years.

I'm getting a cramp in the most peculiar place.

But darling, we can't drink to ourselves!

Well, aren't you going to kiss me?

Only victory will destroy you.

244

I don't think anything will be well received.

I guess we will be openly hostile during the waltz.

There's no limit to jokes.

I'm simply trying to pull you down with me.

I think you're a darling to put up with it.

What if I never tried too hard?

Would that be nice for my gravestone?

"She never tried too hard and she liked it like that."

"She absolutely loved it."

Now look at this tableful of killers.

There's no such thing as being any good.

What is life? An evil cabaret?

I'm going to limp over there and tell you something.

Your crystal dolphin has a crack in it.

Is life only for the winners?

It's my plan to meet that situation by getting well plastered.

Don't you have any extra diamond bracelets lying around?

There's only one sensible thing to do.

That remains to be seen.

246

ACKNOWLEDGMENTS

I'm grateful to Turner Classic Movies. Thanks go to Steve Schmidt for his support, companionship, generosity, and advice. Ruth Tobias deserves thanks for being a brilliant writer, editor, and friend. Thanks to Michele Minnis and Edgar Boles. Thanks to Peter Mayerson. Thanks to Joshua Beckman, Heidi Broadhead, Blyss Ervin, Ryo Yamaguchi, Jeff Clark, and the entire Wave staff for their assistance and professionalism. Special thanks to Charlie Wright. Thank you to all friends and family who have supported me. Thanks to *The Stockholm Review of Literature*, *The Poetry Review*, *Miracle Monocle* (University of Louisville), *New York Tyrant*, *Granta*, *Phoebe* (George Mason University*)*, and *Faultline* (University of California, Irvine) for publishing poems from this book. Thanks to anyone I may have forgotten.

249